A CHARLESTON SKETCHBOOK

A
CHARLESTON
SKETCHBOOK

1796-1806

••••••••••••••••••

*Forty watercolor drawings of
the city and the surrounding country,
including plantations and
parish churches,*

BY

CHARLES FRASER

••••••••••••••••••

With an introduction and notes by
ALICE R. HUGER SMITH

Published for the
CAROLINA ART ASSOCIATION
by the
CHARLES E. TUTTLE COMPANY
Rutland, Vermont

Representatives
Continental Europe: BOXERBOOKS, INC., *Zurich*
British Isles: PRENTICE-HALL INTERNATIONAL, INC., *London*
Australasia: PAUL FLESCH & CO., PTY. LTD., *Melbourne*
Canada: M. G. HURTIG LTD., *Edmonton*

Published by the Charles E. Tuttle Company, Inc.
of Rutland, Vermont & Tokyo, Japan
with editorial offices at
Suido 1-chome, 2-6, Bunkyo-ku, Tokyo, Japan

Copyright in Japan, 1959 by the Carolina Art Association

Library of Congress Catalog Card No. 59-13667

Standard Book No. 8048 0086-3

First edition, 1959
Fifth printing, 1970

PRINTED IN JAPAN

PREFACE

IN THE BIOGRAPHICAL SKETCH IN *The Fraser Gallery*, a catalogue of the 1857 exhibition of Charles Fraser's work, appears the following:

"Here may be seen Charleston as it was, old Plantation residences, and Parish Churches, roughly colored, but with such life and exactness, as to perpetuate many a scene of which there will soon be no trace remaining. This book, closed of course to the public eye in its present form, would be a treasure to an illustrated collection of Southern scenery and residences."

This Sketchbook, presented to Miss Alice R. Huger Smith by Joseph Winthrop, Fraser's greatnephew, was given by her to the Carolina Art Association. We wish to express our appreciation to Miss Smith, and to Miss Ellen M. FitzSimons and the staff of the Charleston Library Society, Miss Mary Frost, Miss Edmonia Martin, and Samuel Gaillard Stoney for their assistance to her in preparing the text for publication. The sketch number 18 was removed by Mr. Fraser and is now lent for inclusion by Miss Elizabeth W. Mitchell.

A bibliography appended at the end of the volume lists all sources consulted. For brevity the sources of the quotations are not always named but the numeral appearing after a quotation refers to the corresponding source in the bibliography and includes all preceding quotations in the same paragraph unless other sources are cited. In the Introduction all quotations are from Fraser's *Reminiscences*.

Robert N. S. Whitelaw, DIRECTOR,
Carolina Art Association

Charleston, South Carolina, 1940

INTRODUCTION

THE PUBLICATION of the more important pages of Charles Fraser's Sketchbook gives pleasure and interest in a form that is delightfully sincere and direct in the utter lack of effort by the artist to impress.

Fraser was but fourteen years of age when he began the book. This accounts for the simplicity of the little watercolor drawings—careful and precise, as was the fashion of the day. A decade covers them, from the first immature efforts to the firmer touch of the later ones.

Historically they induce thought of the weighty events of the years during which they were made, and the still more decisive years then not long past.

Charles Fraser was born in 1782—only a century after the first settlement of Charleston—the hundred years that saw the change from the pioneer's log-house in a vast and unknown country to the homes of an educated and progressive people.

The pioneer life was still fresh in men's minds. Fraser's grandparents had barely escaped with their lives in the great Yemassee War of 1715, when the Indians destroyed the country south of Charles Town to within twenty miles of the city. Yet he, himself, was but a few days old when General Francis Marion fought his last fight; the Revolution was over; and the new state established.

Fraser's *Reminiscences,* published in Charleston in 1854, were written to "be read in private, before an association of literary friends", and give in flowing words a picture of his boyhood, much more stirring than the careful strokes of his brush were able to convey in his youth. Taken together, the sketches and reminiscences complement each other to make a document of great value.

He speaks of the "wagon-yards" for the great wagons from the interior of the state as they came lumbering in with the produce of the country; he quotes from the Harbour Master's reports of January and February, 1797, which give the shipping of those two months as one hundred and eight schooners and sloops; he tells of the Indians "no longer the warlike tribes that had once struck terror amongst the inhabitants of the province" but, in their fallen condition, coming regularly for sales and barter. "There was one who never came to town without a visit to my father, always inquiring after his family, and addressing my mother as sister."

He speaks of tense political moments, usually with such a comment as, "I was present with other boys in the crowd". He tells of the taking down of the marble statue of the Right Hon. William Pitt, put up in 1770 to commemorate "his disinterested and generous assistance towards obtaining a Repeal of the Stamp Act"; a gratitude forgotten in 1794 when the French privateersmen were parading Charleston's streets with long sabres at their sides, and assumed quite an ascendancy in a community then very much in sympathy with the French Revolution.

A little later, however, when the Government was struggling to maintain its neutrality, he says: "I saw the cannon of the old artillery stationed on Beale's wharf, to prevent the sailing of a privateer, which, with her consort, had threatened to batter the city. She remained in the stream an entire day, and then prudently changed her purpose." But when "the awful tragedy of St. Domingo, as is well known, threw upon our shores a crowd of miserable and destitute French, with every claim that humanity could recognize to commiseration and relief, these claims were promptly and honorably answered by the people of Charleston. All who could afford to shelter them, admitted them into their families; whilst all who could not do that, relieved them otherwise readily and cheerfully to the very extent of their means. And it is a recollection, personally gratifying to myself, that I was employed, then a boy, upon errands of charity to those unfortunate beings."

The opposition to Jay's treaty throughout the Union, in 1795, had a violent chapter in Charleston, and the excitement was tremendous. Of course, the young Charles saw much of the "ebullition of popular hatred exhibited on that occasion", but he says when writing about it later, "I have often thought that it was not without its benefit, in giving vent to rankling recollections of the injuries and oppressions sustained by every class of the community, during the Revolutionary struggle then so recently terminated."

He speaks at length of his schooling in the College of Charleston, the charter of which had been granted in 1785. Its buildings were near the ramparts of the Revolutionary fortifications, where the boys used to dig for bullets.

We also find, however, allusion to certain of his activities in "a bill for one term's schooling in which items for books and tuition were mingled with sundry mentions of shillings 'for windows broke'." History and Art are both compelling, but schoolboy life has its own excitements.

The tendencies of Fraser's mind are at once apparent in his Sketchbook. He begins very earnestly with two pen-and-ink drawings, the first of which shows a rock on which is cut a medallion with the head of Washington, and a scroll marked "Liberty" held by the usual Greek figure. On the second page young Fraser gives himself the motto: "E'en Raphael self from rude essays began." But he had put Washington first. Fraser, when nine years old, had seen "the great man" in Charleston, and he never forgot him standing on the steps of the Exchange. Those were the days when the men who had fought long and hard for Independence had embarked on another difficult task; that of building up into a state both great and prosperous a colony ruined by its sacrifices. To quote again from his *Reminiscences:* "from being loyal subjects, they had become a sovereign people with all the obligations of providing for self-government".

In spite of the rigors of poverty that immediately followed the war, the community clung to education and cultivation. Raphael's name appealed to many, and there were other boys also making "rude essays"— notably two of Fraser's friends, Thomas Sully and Washington Allston.

Whilst the Sketchbook was in the making Fraser was beginning to paint miniatures also. Those done in 1802 and 1803 show the excellence and charm of his work before he had attained his majority. The style of the later sketches is in keeping with the viewpoint of the miniature painter; although still minute and delicate, they are much in advance of his earlier efforts.

Their interest now moves from the town to the country, to the homes of his friends, and the views from their houses. Great plantations centred on these dwellings, vigorous industries and enterprises were connected with each name, and the churches represented extensive parishes. Recollections of provincial times were growing dim, and the emotions of the Revolution much less keen. Although Fraser himself never went to England or the Continent, his friends were making frequent trips thereto, and life was on a much easier basis.

In 1800 Malbone, the brilliant young New England miniaturist, was painting in Charleston, and giving Fraser his impetus in that direction, but the latter was also reading law in the office of the Honorable John Julius Pringle, and for these six years until he was admitted to the Bar in 1807, it seems to have been uncertain which profession he would follow. The law won him a competency so in 1818 he could return to the work for which he had always cared most, but a very versatile man, he used his abilities in many directions. His paintings, miniatures and exquisite pencil studies, and his architectural knowledge and writings show how his life was passed in wide cultural activities.

In 1857 many examples of his drawings and paintings were shown in an exhibition in Charleston, which became an ovation to the old man both beloved and admired. The catalogue known as *The Fraser Gallery* remains a source of much information about him. Three hundred and thirteen miniatures were gathered together, and as Charles Fraser looked at the faces which for over fifty years his brush had brought into such a goodly company he must, indeed, have felt again the rush and flow of his times.

The Sketchbook was also shown taking him still farther back into his youth. Now after nearly a century and a half these sketches of his country and his times are being given to the public in the hope that they too may enjoy with young Fraser his first attempts to record the days he spent so pleasurably.

THE SKETCHES

THE SKETCHES

A VIEW OF MR. LINDSAY'S
FROM SOUTH BAY,
MAY 10TH

A VIEW IN CHARLESTON
TAKEN FROM SAVAGE'S GREEN,
1796

In Fraser's *Reminiscences* he tells of the various Greens throughout the town. "There was Savage's Green at the lower end of Broad Street, which, until the building of the old Theatre, was entirely vacant, and spacious enough to be used for military exercise. The old battalion often paraded and fired their pieces there." [3] Fraser remarks that the end of Savage's Green was a favorite swimming place for boys.

Across the creek from the Green "was the town house of Mr. Thomas Ferguson, a large planter of the Parish of St. Paul, and a prominent leader of the Revolutionary party. His house in Charles Town long bore the mark of a British cannon ball fired into the town in 1780." [11]

Next to Ferguson's residence was one owned in 1762 by Rawlins Lowndes. The sketch made by Fraser shows this house—"wooden, with a high hipped roof". [11]

Rawlins Lowndes was in 1778 President of the new state of South Carolina; and Thomas Ferguson held numerous posts, and was in 1780 sent a political prisoner to St. Augustine for his Revolutionary activities.

Ferguson's is the largest house shown in the sketch. It stood until the fire of 1861 just about where Lenwood Street now runs into Tradd Street.

THE SOUTH VIEW OF FORT. MECHANIC
CHARLESTON, JULY 4TH,
1796

Fort Mechanic was built about 1795, when the French "State of War" existed. It was given its name in honour of the mechanics of Charleston who contributed their work voluntarily to its erection. It stood on East Battery, south of the line of the present Atlantic Street. In those days the term "merchants and mechanics" was the equivalent of the "capital and labor" of current times.

The patriotic young Fraser has chosen to show the new fort on the national holiday, flagged up and firing a salute.

The house behind the flagstaff was that of Capt. Missroon built shortly before this period on the walls of Granville's Bastion and now part of the Shriners' Temple. The white house west of the fort is now No. 43 East Battery.

MRS. ROBERT GIBBES' PLACE ON
JOHN'S ISLAND, 1797

The two sea-islands lying southwest of Charles Town were named after two parishes in Barbadoes, St. James and St. John, but they were soon styled James' Island and John's Island.

During the invasion of Prevost "a Hessian battalion occupied the house and plantation of Mr. Robert Gibbes, on the banks of the Stono". Garden's *Anecdotes* gives an account of an attack on them by "two gallies from Charleston ascending the river in the night time". The family set out at midnight for an adjoining plantation but it was "found that in the hurry and terror of the moment, a distant relation, a boy as yet in early infancy, had been left behind". Mr. Gibbes was too infirm to return for him, and the servants refused, but the thirteen-year-old Mary Anna Gibbes went back to rescue the child. "The darkness of the night was profound, yet she returned alone, the distance being fully a mile; and after a long refusal, having by tears and entreaties, obtained permission from the centinel (sic), ascended to the third story. There she found the child, and carried him off in safety, though frequently covered with the dirt thrown up by the shot, and greatly terrified by their constant approach to her person. . . . The gallant Lieutenant Colonel Fenwick, so much distinguished by his services in the late war [1812], was the person saved." [4]

The Gibbes plantation is shown from the river. The outlying buildings or flankers were very characteristic of the larger plantations.

5

CHURCH ON JOHN'S ISLAND

This was St. John's, Colleton, which had been a part of St. Paul's but was separated from it in 1734, and comprised "John's Island, Wadmalaw Island, Edisto Island, and the other adjacent Islands to the seaward".[1] The site chosen was on a part of Mr. Abraham Waight's land.

There were generous donors to the Church, among them George Hext who left twelve hundred and fifty pounds for the Schooling of the Poor Children of the Parish.

In 1770 Colonel John Gibbes; who was a descendant of the Barbadian Churchmen of Goose Creek, left One Thousand Pounds, to be put out with good security, the interest to be used for this Church; and Five Hundred Pounds the interest to be used for the schooling of the Poor Children of the Parish on John's Island; his two sons, Robert and John Gibbes, with the Vestry and Churchwardens, were to act in the matter.

Dalcho says that the Church being in ruins in 1817 a new wooden building was erected by the liberality of Francis Simmons, Esquire.

This sketch in Fraser's book follows immediately that of Mrs. Robert Gibbes' place on John's Island, 1797, so that it may be assumed to have been painted at the same time.

6

THE CHURCH IN
ST. BARTHOLOMEW'S PARISH,
1796

"This part of Colleton County was made a Parish. by an act passed Dec. 18, 1708." [1]

The first missionary, sent by the Society for the Propagation of the Gospel in Foreign Parts to this Parish, was the Reverend Mister Osborn, who arrived in 1713. "His cure was very extensive, and his duty laborious. It was 40 miles long, and 30 wide ... He officiated at five different places for the accommodation of his parishioners ... Mr. Osborn was greatly esteemed and the Church flourished under his care. This prosperity, however, was soon interrupted. In 1715 the Indian War [Yemassee] broke out and the savages destroyed all the plantations in the Parish ... The Missionary with difficulty escaped to Charles Town." [1]

It was long before the Parish recovered from this disaster, but by 1760 two brick Chapels of Ease had been built, the Church shown in this sketch being the Chapel of Pon Pon. It was burnt by the British during the Revolution, but the solid brick walls were rebuilt upon as shown in Fraser's sketch. In 1819 Dalcho speaks of its having been again destroyed by fire and since then the walls, which are still standing, have been known in the countryside as "the Burnt Church".

7

REMAINS OF THE CHURCH IN
PRINCE WILLIAM'S PARISH

This Parish was formerly a part of St. Helena's, having been separated therefrom by an Act of Assembly, May 25, 1745. The Church was often called Sheldon Church because of its proximity to the Bull plantation of that name.

"An instance of the hospitality of Carolina, connected with the history of Sheldon Church, has been stated to us by those who knew the fact. Stephen Bull who lived in its vicinity, usually invited as his guests, on the Sabbath, the more respectable part of the Congregation who attended divine service; while his overseer, by his direction, and at his expense, liberally entertained the rest. At that time, seldom less than 60 or 70 carriages, of various descriptions were seen at the Church on the Lord's Day. It was burnt in 1780 by the British under General Prevost, on their march from Savannah to the siege of Charles-Town." [1] It was rebuilt on its original lines after the Revolution.

In 1864 it was used as a stable by Sherman's troops; and again suffered from the torch of war. Its ruins, therefore, stand today much as they did when Fraser sketched them about 1798.

8

CAPT. FREDERICK FRASER'S PLACE,
PRINCE WILLIAM'S PARISH

In *Prince William's Parish and Plantations* are accounts and maps of "Fraser's Plantation". Its owner at the time this sketch was made was an older brother of the artist. Frederick was the fourth child of Alexander Fraser and Mary Grimké, Charles being the fourteenth.

Alexander was the only son of John Fraser, or John ffrasser, of Wigton, County Galloway, Scotland, who came to Carolina in 1700, and settled near Coosawhatchie in the Indian Lands as a trader with the Yemassee Indians, with whom his relations were most friendly. It was because of a warning from Sanute, a chieftain of the tribe, that he and his wife escaped the general massacre planned by the Spaniards and carried out by the Yemassees and confederated tribes, which occurred on the 15th of April, 1715, and began the Yemassee War. According to family tradition the Frasers had only time hurriedly to reach a boat on a creek whence they made a perilous trip to Charles Town.

9

MEETING-HOUSE IN
PRINCE WILLIAM'S PARISH

This sketch was reproduced in *Prince William's Parish and Plantations*. It was identified with the Stony Creek Presbyterian Church built in Indian Land on Stony Creek near Pocotaligo in 1743. It was destroyed in 1865.

Old Colleton County, which covered that part of the province to the southwest of Charles Town, was very largely settled by the English Dissenters who came in such numbers just before the accession of James II.

Stony Creek Meeting-house was one of their early establishments.

This building is interestingly similar to the Meeting-house near Jacksonborough shown in this volume. Both have the almost ostentatious simplicity affected by the Presbyterians and other "dissenters", who, as Fraser notes in his *Reminiscences,* even during his boyhood never called their places of worship churches.

10

CHURCH IN ST. JAMES' PARISH,
GOOSE CREEK

St. James' Parish, Goose Creek, was laid off in 1706 but the church was not completed until 1719. The surrounding country was known as Goose Creek from the great number of wild fowl, including wild geese, to be found there. In the early days the inhabitants were known as the "Goose Creek men", and their turbulence earned them for awhile a very unfortunate reputation with their government. By 1704 the section was well settled and there was already a Church built by the devotion of the people before the Church Act was passed. An Historical Sketch by Henry A. M. Smith says: "So numerous was the congregation of this church that its capacity was found in a few years wholly insufficient",[18] a Chapel of Ease was erected about seven miles distant which appears to have been destroyed during the Revolutionary War. "The Parish Church was not destroyed. Tradition has it that it was spared because of the fact that above the Chancel there are the Royal Arms of England. It may be that the Chapel of Ease lacked these, or it may be that being on a piece of land which was close to the road, it naturally suffered the fate which we in South Carolina have cause to know accompanies the transit of a hostile army over our soil." [23]

Fraser shows a stuccoed building whose walls have been painted red and whose architectural details were left white, after a fashion still used in the British West Indies.

11

A MEETING-HOUSE NEAR
JACKSONBOROUGH,
1799

This is the meeting-house of Bethel Congregation of Pon Pon organized in St. Bartholomew's Parish in 1728 and first ministered to by the Reverend Archibald Stobo, the Father of Presbyterianism in South Carolina. The old meeting-house according to Howe's *History of the Presbyterian Church in South Carolina* cost under £400 currency. Like the Stony Creek Meeting-house this one lay in Old Colleton County, the Dissenters' country.

Dalcho comments on the Reverend Robert Baron, sent out to St. Bartholomew's Parish by the Society for the Propagation of the Gospel in 1753—"He arrived at Charles Town June 1st and entered on the duties of his cure on the 7th of that month. Mr. Baron was soon after taken ill, and had a severe seasoning, as it is usually called. His Parishioners were scattered over a great extent of country, and were an orderly and well behaved people. The Presbyterians were numerous, but they all lived together in mutual friendship and Christian charity." [1]

The "severe seasoning" touches on the constant toll taken of life, and health, by "country-fever" (malaria). "The sickly season"; the "noxious air of night"; the often expressed wish for frost, which in some interesting letters of 1792 is called "the good Doctor"; the "languishing fever"; these phrases account for information given such as: "Divine Service suspended from June to November"—or "The Parish is abandoned by the inhabitants during the summer months", when every family that could, moved either to "the pines" or "the salt".

12

SHELDON

Fraser's sketch is undated, but was probably made in 1799. Sheldon was then owned by Stephen Bull who had been a Brigadier General of one of the three Brigades of State Militia during the Revolution.

It lay on Huspah Creek in the Indian Lands near the present town of Beaufort, and had been granted to William Bull, son of Stephen Bull who was of the first ship's company of Emigrants to Charles Town. It became in time one of the richest plantations of a rich neighborhood.

At its beginning it was the scene of a pioneer tragedy. Colonel John Bull, a younger brother of William, there lost his first wife at the opening of the Yemassee War. One account says that while in his fields he saw smoke in the direction of his dwelling. Hastening there he found his house in flames, his wife missing. Her negro maid told him that the Indians had attacked the place, that she had succeeded in hiding in the bushes, but her mistress had been carried off. The poor woman was never heard of again, but some bones and a silver shoe-buckle were found that were supposed to be hers.

13

VIEW FROM
MR. FRASER'S CITY RESIDENCE,
1796

Alexander Fraser's mother lived at 25 King Street during her widowhood. This house would seem to be the same in which Fraser lived, and where working in a northeast room directly on the street he painted most of his miniatures.

It was probably from this old house (now 55 King Street) that this view was taken. There are still wooden houses nearly opposite which very much resemble those shown in this sketch.

This was the Tavern made famous by the important
Battle of Eutaw Springs in 1781, between the Americans under General Greene and the British under
Colonel Alexander Stuart. The battle with its fortunes
varying in favor between the opposing forces, surged
around this two-story brick house, "abundantly strong
to resist small arms" and commanding adjacent fields.
The victory was claimed by both sides with equal
foundation for the assertion. "The first and immediate
results were clearly with the British", but "the ultimate
advantages were with the Americans, for while the
losses were great on both sides, the waning power of
the British could less afford the great loss of this
bloody and hard-fought action." [7]

The Tavern has long since disappeared, but at
Eutaw Plantation some of the bricks in the arched
foundations of the piazza were brought from its ruins.

Nearby are the beautiful springs of limestone water
which form Eutaw Creek and spread into the cypress
swamps so enchanting in their loveliness.

15

THE CHURCH
IN ST. ANDREW'S PARISH,
APRIL, 1800

Established in 1706, by 1722 the Church proved too small for the congregation and was enlarged in the form of a cross, with a gallery at the west end which was used by "people of colour". Destroyed by fire, it was rebuilt by subscription in 1764. It is this building that is shown in Fraser's sketch. Extending as it did up the west bank of the Ashley River St. Andrew's Parish included many of the important early plantations—among them Ashley Hall. Like most of the Parishes it covered a great territory. It had a Chapel of Ease on James' Island, which was attended also by many Presbyterian families of that Island, but, after 1787, the Reverend Thomas Mills states that "the inhabitants of James Island, who were nearly all Presbyterians, or Independents, had procured a minister and organized a Church of their own. After this period, in conformity with the injunctions of the Vestry, my Pastoral duties were generally confined to St. Andrew's on the main." [1] It is interesting to find from the early accounts and reports of these Parishes of the Church of England, how interwoven they were with other denominations.

St. Andrew's Church, looking much as it did on the day when young Fraser sketched it, is easily seen from the road that leads from Charleston to Middleton Place.

VIEW OF A PLANTATION BARN

It seems impossible to identify this building. It can therefore merely be noted as an example of the substantial, often handsome, architecture applied to the offices and outbuildings both of the Charleston residences and of the plantation settlements in the Low Country.

A VIEW OF ST. JAMES' CHURCH, GOOSE CREEK, FROM THE PARSONAGE

When this sketch was made about 1800, the rector was the Reverend Milward Pogson. There are many good stories about Church and Parsonage. One is of the stormy courtship of Mad Archy Campbell, Lieutenant Colonel of the 71st British Regiment, who took lovely Miss Paulina Philp to drive in his gig; his fast trotting horse getting them to Goose Creek from Charleston in short order. A pistol at the head of Mr. Ellington, the rector at the time, and a half fainting bride figure in the story, as gossip had it, but a descendant of the pair denied this absolutely, saying that the lady, far from fainting, was entirely willing, and that it was her grandmother who objected to the match.

The parsonage stood on a slight hill which is at the northeast of the present road where it curves towards the Church. There are still vestiges of the older road shown in this sketch which, after a well established Low Country custom, led squarely to a door of the Church. Just beyond the gig, in the woods you may see a small vestry building where Parish business could be transacted, and where in cold or bad weather coachmen and grooms might take shelter. This vestry room was built in 1759 by Mr. Thomas Wright at his own expense for the Parish. The foundations of this building are now just in front of the sexton's house.

18

THE SEAT OF
JOHN JULIUS PRINGLE, ESQ.,
ON ASHLEY RIVER,
1800

The original tract of Runnymede with other lands was granted to John Cattell, remaining in that family until 1777. It passed in 1795 to John Julius Pringle. The Duke de la Rochefoucault Liancourt who spent some time with him in Charleston tells of a trip up the Ashley River—"we crossed the River, and stopped at a plantation lately purchased by Mr. Pringle, the former name of which was Greenville, but which he has named 'Susan's Place' in honour of his lovely wife . . . The new mansion . . . will be finished this summer." [17] Mr. Pringle ultimately named the place "Runnymede".

John Julius Pringle read law in the office of John Rutledge, later becoming a student in the Temple. Whilst there his letters and articles written in the cause of his country attracted notice. Going over to France he became secretary to Ralph Izard, first Commissioner to the Court of Tuscany. When he returned to Carolina he entered on a long career of legal and political prominence. In 1792 he became Attorney General of South Carolina, declining the Attorney Generalship of the United States in 1805, when offered that post by Jefferson. He died in 1843, aged ninety. It was in Mr. Pringle's office that Charles Fraser began to read law in 1804.

19

THE SEAT OF
JOSEPH WINTHROP, ESQ.,
GOOSE CREEK

Charles Fraser must have spent many days at this plantation, Mr. Winthrop having married Fraser's elder sister Mary.

The lady fishing gaily up the stream, and the gentleman disconsolately fishing down the stream, with the tree between them, evidently carried amusement to the onlooker on the steps of the house, perhaps Fraser himself.

Mrs. Winthrop had been left by her father a portion of the plantation known as Wigton, her brother James owning the rest. Her part seems to have gone by the name of Brighton. This plantation and its neighbors were in easy reach from Charleston on the road, and therefore very popular places for occasional visits.

20

MR. GABRIEL MANIGAULT'S SEAT
AT GOOSE CREEK,
1802

This estate, called Steepbrook, lay next to Brighton and Wigton. It was one of the many owned by the Manigaults and was used by them as the contemporary equivalent of our week-end cottages. Mrs. Anne Manigault's diary constantly notes visits of her family to Goose Creek, in the 1760's and 1770's.

The *South Carolina Gazette* of November 10th, 1766, says that on "the Anniversary of the glorious Revolution, by the landing of King William and the nation's happy deliverance from a horrid Popish Plot, the same was observed here with suitable demonstrations of joy. The hon. Peter Manigault, Esq., Speaker of the Commons House of Assembly, gave upon this occasion, an elegant entertainment to the Light Infantry Company, at his Seat at Goose Creek, 14 miles from Charles Town, where the company arrived at 7 o'clock in the morning, Spent the day most agreeably, and returned before 9 at night."

Peter Manigault studied law at the Inner Temple. His public life in Carolina is a matter of history, he being the very active Speaker of the Commons House during the troubles following the Stamp Act. He died before the Revolution broke out, but his father and son shouldered muskets together on the walls of Charlestown. It was this son, Gabriel Manigault, who was the owner of Steepbrook at the time of Fraser's sketch. Peter Manigault's father, also a Gabriel, was a very successful merchant and planter, although the previous generation of his Huguenot family had fled from France utterly without resources.

THE SEAT OF JAMES FRASER, ESQ.,
GOOSE CREEK

This James Fraser was an elder brother of Charles. Their father seems to have been an extensive land-owner, with many other plantations besides this Goose Creek place. It was named Wigton, from the town Wigton in Scotland, whence the family had come.

A VIEW NEAR CHARLESTON, 1801.

WHERE ST. PAUL'S CHURCH NOW STANDS.

RATCLIFFE LANDS.

Charles Town at the end of the peninsula between the Ashley and Cooper Rivers gradually absorbed the various boroughs and villages that had sprung up beyond its walls.

Ratcliffe or Radcliffeboro was one of these. The Church which now stands where this sketch was made is a distinguished building of the early nineteenth century. It still keeps alive the name of the old neighborhood, as it was always called St. Paul's, Radcliffeboro.

Another was Ansonboro laid out in 1746 on lands belonging to George, Lord Anson, the famous sailor who had just circumnavigated the globe. Two of the streets were named after him and are still known as George and Anson Streets, but those named after the *Centurion,* "the famous ship in which he made that famous voyage" around the world, the *Scarborough,* in which he was long stationed on this coast, and the *Squirrel,* his second ship also sent to Carolina, have all been changed. Mazyckboro, where stood the famous Liberty Tree; Middlesex, laid out by General Gadsden—in which was Hand-in-Hand Corner; Wraggboro, where the streets were named after Mr. Wragg's sons and daughters, Elizabeth, Charlotte, John, Alexander, etc.; Harleston and Cannonsboro, where the windmill is shown in one of these sketches; Hampstead with its Mall, an enterprise of Henry Laurens; the names of all these and others were long used in common parlance to distinguish portions of the city.

NEAR CHARLESTON, JUNE, 1805

A VIEW NEAR CHARLESTON,
1802

"A large part of Harleston (a village) and more es-
pecially the lots bordering upon the low ground and
marshes of Coming's Creek, was early acquired by Mr.
Thomas Bennett Sr., who, with Daniel Cannon, utilized
the ebb and flow of the tides by establishing on these
waters large lumber mills. This tidal power was also
used largely upon the rice-growing rivers for pounding
mills, which separated the husk from the grain; . . .
Nor was it only the waterpower which was utilized,
for among the lots conveyed in 1804 by Thomas Bennett Sr. to Thomas Bennett, Jr., later Governor of
South Carolina, was the lot of marshland on which the
windmill stood near by a branch of Coming's Creek." [11]
In the *Charleston Courier* December 15, 1825, ap-
peared a notice: "At Private Sale . . . that large Brick
Wind Mill, situate on Harleston's Green, adapted for
the sawing of lumber". Windmills, and watermills with
vast undershot wheels, worked by the tides, were
common in the neighborhood along the Ashley.

25

A SEAT ON ASHLEY RIVER,
APRIL, 1802

The house in this sketch unfortunately cannot be identified. It is typical of much plantation architecture, and that of the West Indies, in having a basement story of masonry, and the upper one of wood. The double stairway to the semi-classic porch is also very characteristic of this country. This house may have been one of the Cattell residences where Fraser as a cousin was a familiar guest.

26

ASHLEY HALL, 1803

This was one of the first plantations in the Colony, and its history is continuously interesting. Stephen Bull came to Carolina with the first ship in 1669-70 as Lord Ashley's deputy, and the following year settled Ashley Hall on the Ashley River. He assisted in selecting the site of Charles Town, and played a prominent part in the Colony's beginnings. He was a great explorer among the Indians, and was chosen Caseeka of the Etiwans. His eldest son, William, inherited Ashley Hall. Fraser says in his *Reminiscences* that the oak trees were planted by a visitor, Mark Catesby, who came to Carolina in 1722, and whose *Natural History of Carolina, Florida, and the Bahama Islands* was published in England a decade later.

William Bull was even more important than his father, both in civil and military life. A loyal supporter of the Lords Proprietors, in the Revolution of 1719, he became under the Crown a member of the King's Council of South Carolina, and was appointed to assist General Oglethorpe in settling Georgia. As Lieutenant Governor of the Province his administration was marked by war, pestilence, and famine, but he overcame all difficulties. His influence kept the Indians quiet; he suppressed an insurrection; and he raised forces against the Spaniards. Besides the lands inherited from his father he had large grants in Prince William's Parish, where he settled the Sheldon estate, helping to erect the Church. He died there in 1755.

His second son, William, continued the tradition of his father and grandfather. His life is told in connection with the sketch following.

27

ANOTHER VIEW OF ASHLEY HALL,
1803

The second Governor William Bull inherited Ashley Hall in 1755. The first American to graduate in medicine in Europe (Leyden, 1734) he returned to Carolina, becoming five times Lieutenant Governor of the Province, filling the post with notable success. He never wavered in his loyalty and duty to his King, and his character was such that it was thought that if he had been Governor in that crisis the Revolution in South Carolina might have been averted. He left with the British in 1782, dying in London nine years later. His will reflects the times: "I William Bull the late Governour of South Carolina for his Brittanic Majesty do ... my worldly goods greatly deranged and lessened in value not by my Fault but by some unexpected contingencies I have met from peculiar situations wherein I have been placed during the late unhappy times in America ... my plantation on Ashley River in Carolina where my Grandfather lived died and lies buried where my Father and all his children were born I wish to remain in the possession of one of his Posterity I therefore give to my nephew William his heirs ..." [13] His nephew, the third William Bull, had himself led an active life in the Revolutionary party. He died in 1805, two years after this sketch was painted by Fraser.

The previous sketch shows an obelisk erected by his widow to this second Governor Bull. It carries his portrait in bas-relief.

28

A VIEW IN ST. THOMAS' PARISH
POMPION HILL CHAPEL

The Parish of St. Thomas and St. Dennis was made from the union of the Huguenot Church St. Denis and the Parish of St. Thomas which had been laid off by the Church Act of 1706.

Irving in his *Day on Cooper River* says: "on a high bluff, rising abruptly from the bed of the river, stands the Parish Chapel, commonly known as Pompion Hill Chapel, taking its name from the hill on which it stands." [6] Locally the pronunciation soon became "Punkin Hill". This building was finished in 1765. The plan of the Church is unusual—the Pulpit being at the western end opposite the Chancel, whilst the benches face the aisle that runs between the two. A note on the margin of the sketch by Fraser says that it was "taken from Mr. Lucas's mills". Jonathan Lucas married Lydia Simons of Middleburg, she inheriting in 1789 the part of the plantation containing the settlement and most of the waterfront. Mr. Lucas had given a great impetus to the rice-planting industry by the introduction of water-mills. The first of these was put up by him in 1787 at Mr. Bowman's Santee plantation.

Washington Allston in speaking of Mr. Bowman says: "Malbone, Fraser, and myself were frequent guests at his table, and delightful parties we always found there." [12]

29

A BASON AND STOREHOUSE BELONGING
TO THE SANTEE CANAL,
1803

This was identified by the late Thomas Porcher
Ravenel as the Storehouse at Simpson's Lock. Profes-
sor F. A. Porcher tells us that in 1786 a company had
been chartered for a canal between the Santee and
Cooper Rivers but that the work was not begun until
1793. "Doubtless the pressure of the times retarded
the commencement of operations. Late in 1800, perhaps not before the end of December, the canal was
opened for the passage of boats from river to river".[9]
He says that when finished the canal had cost more
than thirty thousand dollars a mile—the distance being
twenty-two miles. Governor John Rutledge and his
brother Governor Edward Rutledge were among the
incorporators, and as Fraser apparently made this
sketch during his visits to Richmond, the home of
Edward Rutledge the younger, his interest in this
Lock is easily accounted for. It was expected that a
town would be built at Simpson's which lay under a
high hill with a large basin for the accommodation
of boats. The canal throve until it was superseded by
the railways.

30

RICE HOPE,
THE SEAT OF DR. WILLIAM READ
ON THE COOPER RIVER

Rice Hope lies not far from Strawberry Ferry, at the old "Childsbury Township, where the British forces in the Keowe expedition [against the Cherokees] were landed from the transports, and marched under Governor Littleton". This quotation from Irving's *Day on Cooper River* gives one of the early historical happenings in that part of the country. Later on Rice Hope saw the stress of the Revolution, but in 1795 Dr. William Read was banking and clearing it for the new tidal cultivation of rice. It had come into his possession through his marriage with Miss Sarah Harleston.

Dr. Read had been a Physician and Surgeon in the Continental Line, and Irving says there were many anecdotes about his Revolutionary services, and pleasant personality.

The name Rice Hope was one of the many such combinations; there were also a Silk Hope, a Salt Hope, and a Brick Hope in the Cooper River country, or near it.

31

RICE HOPE,

TAKEN FROM ONE OF THE

RICE FIELDS

Dr. Henry Woodward is credited with having first procured and dispersed for planting Gold Seed Rice from Madagascar about 1685. By 1690 the production of rice in South Carolina had so advanced that the planters asked that it might be specified as one of the commodities in which they might pay their quit-rents. By 1700 its production was declared by the Collector of Customs to have been so great that there had not been enough ships in Charles Town that year in which to export it all.

The scheme of tidal cultivation depended on banking the silt in the wide river beds by a system of ditches, banks and flood-gates. The method was expensive but the rewards were superlative and the river bottom fields could produce bumper crops without manuring. The most onerous part of making a crop had always been husking which was not mechanized until about 1790 when Jonathan Lucas set up the first successful rice-pounding mill in the Low Country.

Fraser's sketch shows tidal rice fields lately developed on an already old rice river.

32

RICHMOND, THE SEAT OF
EDWARD RUTLEDGE, ESQ., IN ST. JOHN'S PARISH,
1803

The Richmond house stood on a fine hill overlooking the Eastern branch of the Cooper River, just across from Pompion Hill Chapel. It had belonged to Colonel John Harleston, of one of the oldest Cooper River families. From him it had passed to his daughter Jane Smith Harleston, the wife of Edward Rutledge, whom she married in 1794.

The house at Richmond is one of the most typical Low Country plantation houses sketched by Fraser. On any rice river or sea island just such four-square and ample buildings might have been found years before the artist was born and many of them stand at present.

The high foundation of masonry, the two stories of wood, the high hipped roof, the single piazza with its wide brick stairway flanked by ramps of the same material that flare out at the ground into cylindrical newels—all these repeat themselves endlessly through the Low Country, with only minor local variations.

At Richmond, too, Charles Fraser found himself on one of the truly rich plantations of the Low Country. The Harlestons who had inherited land on Cooper River from two of the settlers who had come on the first ship, the *Carolina*, were a great family of planters. In their hands and those of their connections well placed plantations like Richmond (where twenty acres once averaged a crop of ninety bushels) made ample fortunes for their lucky possessors.

The house shown in this sketch long survived only to be burnt at last accidentally about the end of the last century.

33

ANOTHER VIEW OF RICHMOND,
MAY, 1803

The three sketches of Richmond found their way very naturally into Fraser's "vade mecum" as he called his little Sketchbook. Mr. Edward Rutledge was his first cousin.

Governor John Rutledge had married an aunt of Charles Fraser's; the latter therefore grew up in intimate knowledge of the stirring events of Rutledge's remarkable career which placed him from his genius and rectitude among the greatest of Americans.

34

A VIEW ON RICHMOND,
1805

O'Neall's account of Fraser in his *Bench and Bar* says: "When at school he was a favorite of our great Chief Justice, the Honorable John Rutledge—the guiding star of our state, during the darkest days of the Revolution",[8] and adds that Fraser looked up with veneration to him and learned from his own lips much of the history of our country. Fraser in his *Reminiscences* often makes allusion to meetings and conversations which carry great interest. History cannot be re-written here but the election of John Rutledge to the Presidency of South Carolina in 1776 and to the Governorship under a new Constitution in 1779, cannot be omitted, culminating as they did in 1780 when the Assembly found it necessary to adjourn, but first delegated "till ten days after their next session to the Governor, John Rutledge, Esquire, and such of the Council as he could conveniently consult, a power to do everything necessary to the public good except the taking away the life of a citizen without a legal trial."[7] With these powers he carried the War in South Carolina to a successful conclusion.

The memory of these events of vital importance underlay the return of prosperity to the country, and the busy renewal of mercantile and planting activities. The Cooper River plantations were among those that were forging ahead at this period of Fraser's life, and his visits to relatives in that section help to make the great interest of the Sketchbook.

35

MEPKIN,
THE SEAT OF HENRY LAURENS, ESQ.

Mepkin was among the several tracts of land granted at the very commencement of the Colony to the three sons of Sir John Colleton, one of the eight Lords Proprietors. It comprised 3,000 acres and lay nearly opposite Mepshew (now Pimlico), another grant of the three brothers.

John Colleton of the County of Middlesex, England, sold Mepkin in 1762 to Henry Laurens. Vital affairs of the Colony, of the Revolution, and of the new state, all had a hearing there. After the destruction of the house during the Revolution Henry Laurens built the one that is shown in the sketch, and in which Henry Laurens, Jr., was living. As the latter had married a daughter of John Rutledge, Fraser was again among relatives, seeing familiarly a scene where history was made.

36

ANOTHER VIEW OF MEPKIN,

MAY, 1803

McCrady in his summing up of the careers of
Henry Laurens and his son John, says: "They were
the most conspicuous figures from South Carolina in
and near the Congressional government during the
Revolution." [7] He goes on to say that whilst John Rutledge was carrying on the state activities, when
through captivity or death the delegates who had
taken so prominent a part in Congress prior to the
Declaration of Independenee were no longer present
in its hall, Laurens was taking a high and leading posi-
tion as President of Congress during the eventful year
of 1777-78. His captivity in the Tower of London followed, with his exchange for Cornwallis after York-
town, and his association with Franklin, Jay and
Adams in the signing of the Treaty of Peace.

His son, Colonel John Laurens, was scarcely less
distinguished than his father, combining with political prominence a fine military record. He was killed
in the last skirmish of the Revolution in South Carolina.

Henry Laurens lived until 1792, a little over a
decade before this sketch was made.

37

A VIEW ON MEPKIN

The Avenue at Mepkin leads from the road along wooded ravines to the bluff close by the river, overlooking the rice-fields and the winding stream. There stood the house of Henry Laurens. Mepkin had great natural beauties, and throughout his life Henry Laurens had added to these by continuous attention to the possibilities of agriculture in South Carolina.

In connection with this, the following quotation from David Ramsay's *History of South Carolina* is interesting. He describes the extensive garden of Laurens' house in Charlestown: "enriched with everything useful and ornamental that Carolina produced or his extensive mercantile connexion enabled him to procure from remote parts of the world. Among the variety of other curious productions he introduced olives, capers, limes, ginger, guinea grass, the Alpine strawberry, bearing nine months in the year, red raspberries, blue grapes; and also, directly from the South of France, apples, pears, and plums of fine kinds, and vines which bore abundantly of the choicest white eating grape called Chasselats blancs." [10]

38

BRABANTS ON FRENCH QUARTER CREEK,
APRIL 18, 1800.
THE SEAT OF THE LATE
BISHOP SMITH

This plantation lies on French Quarter Creek, a tributary of the Eastern Branch of the Cooper River. The basis was an original grant to Francis Pagett in 1704, to which was later joined a tract granted in 1709 to Daniel Brabant, a surgeon whose name became that of the plantation. It amounted to 3,000 acres when Elizabeth Pagett married the Reverend Robert Smith, rector of St. Philip's Church in Charles Town. Mr. Smith extended and developed it greatly. There are many Revolutionary stories told about the place, and about him, he being an ardent supporter of the Revolution. His name is the first mentioned in the list of those whose property was confiscated by Sir Henry Clinton's order.

After the War he re-occupied Brabant as his country seat when his duties in Charleston permitted He became the first Bishop of the State of South Carolina, and was the First Principal of the College of Charleston—Charles Fraser was one of the students, and he and Bishop Smith's two sons were firm friends throughout their lives.

The visit marked by this sketch must have been soon after Bishop Smith's death in 1800.

ANOTHER VIEW OF
BRABANTS

Brabant, or Brabants, has been described as having a fine garden, shrubbery, and ornamental lake. Although all traces of the settlement have gone the pool, grown up with reeds and cypress, was long known as "the Bishop's fishpond".

A SOUTHWEST VIEW OF NEWPORT

Mr. Fraser made many trips to the northern states, the first, apparently, being in 1806. A letter dated October 9th tells of a visit in August or September of that year to Newport. There he saw Malbone: "Poor Malbone is not in a condition to paint. I am afraid that he is hastening to that bourne whence no traveller can return. He was ill the whole time I remained in Newport." [12] Fraser seems to have paid many pleasant visits and seen a great deal of that part of the country. Many of his larger paintings show scenes in New England, New York, and elsewhere, but this is the only drawing in the Sketchbook that is definitely so named.

Newport was then an old established summering place for South Carolinians. There was also a considerable trade connection between the town and Charleston—the one a city of shipowners and the other of cargoes. Young Malbone as a rising artist had come naturally from his native Newport to Charleston· young Fraser as naturally returned the visit.